# Brief Explanation of the Words of Salah

## By
## Rameez Abid

Dhu'l-Qi'dah 1441 | July 2020

Messenger of Allah ﷺ is reported to have said:

إِنَّ أَوَّلَ مَا يُحَاسَبُ بِهِ الْعَبْدُ يَوْمَ الْقِيَامَةِ صَلاَتُهُ فَإِنْ وُجِدَتْ تَامَّةً كُتِبَتْ
تَامَّةً وَإِنْ كَانَ انْتَقَصَ مِنْهَا شَىْءٌ قَالَ انْظُرُوا هَلْ تَجِدُونَ لَهُ مِنْ تَطَوُّعٍ
يُكَمِّلُ لَهُ مَا ضَيَّعَ مِنْ فَرِيضَةٍ مِنْ تَطَوُّعِهِ ثُمَّ سَائِرُ الأَعْمَالِ تَجْرِي عَلَى
حَسَبِ ذَلِكَ

*"The first thing for which a person will be brought to account
on the Day of Resurrection will be his prayer (salah). If it is
found to be complete then it will be recorded as complete,
and if anything is lacking, Allah will say: 'Look and see if you
can find any voluntary prayers with which to complete what
he neglected of his obligatory prayers.' Then the rest of his
deeds will be reckoned in like manner."*

(Reported by an-Nasai)

# Table of Contents

Introduction                                           4

Takbeer                                                6

Istiftaah (The Opening)                                7

Ta'awwuz (Seeking Refuge)                              9

Basmala                                                11

Al-Fatihah                                             13

Ruku' (The Bowing)                                     17

Rising From Ruku'                                      18

Sujood (The Prostration)                               19

Tashahhud (The Sitting)                                20

   First Part                           20

   Second Part                          23

   Third Part                           25

Common Mistakes During Salah                           28

Further Useful Resources on Salah                      30

# Introduction

The five daily prayers are a fundamental part of Islamic lifestyle. It is one of the five pillars of Islam as mentioned in the *hadith* of Ibn Umar that the Messenger of Allah ﷺ said:

بُنِيَ الإِسْلَامُ عَلَى خَمْسٍ شَهَادَةِ أَنْ لاَ إِلَهَ إِلاَّ اللهُ وَأَنَّ مُحَمَّدًا عَبْدُهُ وَرَسُولُهُ وَإِقَامِ الصَّلاَةِ وَإِيتَاءِ الزَّكَاةِ وَحَجِّ الْبَيْتِ وَصَوْمِ رَمَضَانَ

*"Islam is based on five: testifying (the fact) that there is no deity worthy of worship but Allah and Muhammad is His servant and messenger, **the establishment of prayer**, payment of zakat, pilgrimage to the House (Ka'ba) and the fast of Ramadan."*

(Reported by Muslim)

However, the sad reality is that most Muslims do not understand what they are saying in Arabic to their Lord. This leads to their daily prayers feeling more like chores than a real connection with their Maker. In this brief book, I intend to explain every expression used in the prayer so that they no longer remain just empty words but phrases with real intended meanings.

I have intentionally kept this work small and to the point so that it can be quickly read and reviewed on a regular basis to integrate the meanings of the words of *salah* (prayer) in the reader's mind. I hope that through it, the reader can learn to build a real connection with Allah in his/her prayer and find real peace and tranquility in his/her worship.

Please note that I use the words 'salah' and 'prayer' interchangeably throughout the text.

# Takbeer

The *takbeer* is repeated throughout the prayer. The prayer is started by its utterance and the different postures in prayer are shifted by it. It is also the most common phrase in the prayer:

الله أكبر

*Allaahu Akbar*

Allah is Greater

It means Allah is **Greater** than everything else, not just in your life but the entire existence. There is nothing greater and more important than Him. If He is pleased with you but everyone else displeased, then you have nothing to fear. If He is displeased with you but everyone else is pleased, then you have everything to fear.

# Istiftaah (The Opening)

There are different supplications reported in the *hadith* literature that can be read for this part of the prayer, but the following one is the most commonly recited among the people, therefore, I will stick to it alone.

سبحانك اللهم وبحمدك، وتبارك اسمك، وتعالى جدك، ولا إله غيرك

*Subhaanaka Allaahumma wabi hamdika wa tabaarakasmuka wa ta'aala jadduka wa laa ilaaha ghayruka*

*How perfect You are, O Allah, and with You is all [types of] praise. Blessed be Your name, lofty is Your position, and none has the right to be worshiped except You*

سبحانك اللهم

## How perfect You are, O Allah

*It means how sacred You are, O Allah, and free from every type of deficiency and defect.*

و بحمدك

## And with You is all [types of] praise

*It means all praise and thanks belong to You alone because You are the Originator of everything. When we praise anything in existence, we are indirectly praising Allah as well because He is the Creator of everything.*

و تبارك اسمك

## Blessed be Your name

*It means glorified and respectable is Your name and abundantly blessed.*

و تعالى جدك

## Lofty is Your position

*It means Your greatness and power, O Allah, are elevated and ascended.*

ولا إله غيرك

## None has the right to be worshiped except You

*It means there is no deity worthy of worship other than You.*

# Ta'awwuz (Seeking Refuge)

Allah has legislated for every reciter of the Qur'an to seek refuge with Him from the expelled *Shaytan* (Satan) before beginning the recitation of His final book. Allah said,

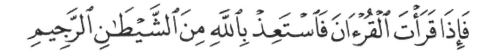

**So when you recite the Qur'an, [first] seek refuge in Allah from Satan, the expelled [from His mercy]**

[Qur'an 16:98]

That is because the Qur'an is a guidance for mankind and a cure for what is in the hearts. Satan is a means to evils and misguidance, therefore, Allah commanded every reciter of the Qur'an to seek protection in Him from Satan, his whispers, and his party.

Since the worshiper is about to start reciting the Qur'an, it is befitting that he recite the *ta'wwuz* before moving forward.

أعوذ بالله من الشيطان الرجيم

*A'oodhu billaahi minash-Shaytaanir-rajeem*

*I seek refuge in Allah from the expelled Shaytan*

أعوذ بالله

**I seek refuge in Allah**

*Meaning I seek protection/recourse in Allah alone.*

من الشيطان

## From the *Shaytan* (Satan)

*Meaning from every rebellious and arrogant being from among the jinn and mankind that diverts me from obeying my Lord and reciting His book.*

الرجيم

## The expelled

*Meaning the one who is expelled or ousted from every type of good. Since Satan has been expelled from Allah's mercy for eternity, he is often designated by this title. It is also often translated as 'cursed'.*

# Basmala

The *basmala* is the popular phrase that every Muslim, young and old, recognizes and uses in his/her daily life.

بسم الله الرحمن الرحيم

*Bismillaahhir-Rahmaanir-Raheem*

*In the name of Allah, the Entirely Merciful, the Especially Merciful*

This is recited before the beginning of every chapter of the Qur'an except *Surah al-Tawbah*. We are reciting it here because of *Surah al-Fatihah*, which follows immediately after it.

بسم الله

## In the Name of Allah

*Meaning I begin with the name of Allah seeking His help with being able to read this book with success and acceptance from Him.*

*'Allah' is a known name in the Arabic language in reference to the Lord of the entire universe. It is also among the names of Allah that are specific to Him and cannot be given to anyone other than Him.*

الرحمن

## The Entirely Merciful

*'Ar-Rahmaan' (Entirely Merciful) is one of the names of Allah and it means that His mercy expands over all of His creation. It is a more general form of mercy which extends to the entire creation.*

الرحيم

## The Especially Merciful

*Ar-Raheem' (Especially Merciful) is also one of the names of Allah and it means a form of mercy from Him reserved specifically for the believers.*

# Al-Fatihah[1]

*Al-Fatihah* literally means **the opening** because the Qur'an opens with it. This is also the first chapter (*surah*) of the Qur'an and is considered its 'greatest *surah*'. It is seen to be a precise table of contents of the Qur'anic message because scholars of exegesis have stated that this chapter is a summary of the entire Qur'an.

Its seven verses are regularly recited at the start of every unit (*rak'ah*) of the prayer and this is why one of its names is **The Seven Oft-Repeated Verses**. The five daily prayers without it are considered invalid. It has other names as well, such as, the **Mother of the Book**, **The Cure**, **The Commendation (*Hamd*)**, and many others.

**[All] praise is [due] to Allah, Lord of the worlds**

*Allah attributes all forms of praise to Himself. This includes praiseworthy actions done by His slaves because He alone is truly entitled to it as He is the Originator of all creation, the true Executor of their affairs. He takes care of all His creation through His innumerable favors and especially takes care of His awliyaah (supporters) by keeping them firm on true faith and righteous actions.*

---

[1] The explanation provided for this *surah* here is primarily based on the highly popular Qur'anic exegesis published in Arabic called *al-Tafseer al-Muyassar*, which was prepared by a selected group of scholars.

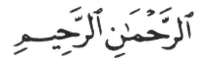

## The Entirely Merciful, the Especially Merciful

*Ar-Rahmaan' (Entirely Merciful) is one of the names of Allah and it means that His mercy expands over all His creation. Ar-Raheem' (Especially Merciful) is also one of the names of Allah and it means a form of mercy from Him reserved specifically for the believers.*

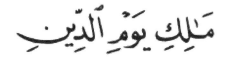

## Master of the Day of Judgement

*He alone is the Master of the Day of Resurrection. It is the Day of Recompense for deeds in this life. Some will be rewarded through His Mercy while others punished through His Justice. Allah specifically mentions His sovereignty alone on the Day of Judgement in this verse because no one will claim anything on that day and no one will be allowed to speak except by His permission.*

*Reading this verse in every unit (rak'ah) of the daily prayer should remind the Muslim of the Last Day and encourage him/her to prepare righteous deeds and abstain from sins.*

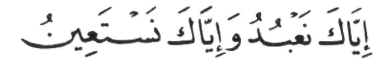

**It is You alone we worship and You alone we ask for help**

*Meaning it is You alone to whom we give our complete obedience and worship. And we seek Your help alone in all of our affairs, because everything is in Your hands and no one else has any dominion over it at all.*

**Guide us to the straight path**

*Meaning show us and guide us to the straight path and keep us firm on it until we meet You. This straight path is Islam, which leads to the pleasure of Allah and to His paradise. It is a path which was shown to us by the seal of the prophets, Muhammad ﷺ. No other way will lead to happiness for the slave except remaining steadfast on this single straight path.*

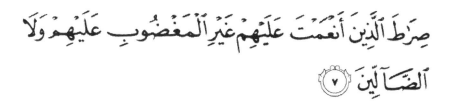

**The path of those upon whom You have bestowed favor, not of those who have evoked [Your] anger or of those who are astray**

*Meaning the path of those whom You have favored, such as, the prophets, the truthful ones, the martyrs, and the righteous. They are people of guidance and steadfastness. In addition, there is protection sought from two types of people:*

- *To not make us among those who took the path of evoking His anger. They are those who knew the truth but did not act in accordance to it.*
- *To not make us among those who went astray due to lack of knowledge. They are those who were not guided so they went astray from the straight path by acting without knowledge.*

After the *Al-Fatihah*, the person can recite any chapter of the Qur'an in its entirety or just a part of it. Due to the fact that this varies from person to person, I have not included an explanation for other chapters of the Qur'an in this small booklet.

# Ruku' (The Bowing)

The phrase below is uttered during the bowing posture. It is a show of humility and submissiveness to Allah.

سبحان ربي العظيم

*Subhaana Rabbi-yal Azeem*

*How perfect is my Lord, the Most Supreme*

سبحان ربي

## How perfect is my Lord

*Meaning my Lord, who created me and sustains me, is sacred and free from all forms of deficiencies and defects.*

العظيم

## The Most Supreme

*Meaning He is the greatest in power, loftiness, sanctity, and everything else.*

# Rising From Ruku'

This is the posture right after the bowing when the worshiper stands erect back to the standing posture.

سمع الله لمن حمده ربنا ولك الحمد

*Sami'a Allaahu liman hamidah, Rabbanaa walakal hamd*

*Allah hears the one who praises Him. Our Lord! All praise is due only to You*

سمع الله لمن حمده

## Allah hears the one who praises Him

*Meaning O Allah! Hear me praise You. Hear it, accept it, and answer it.*

ربنا ولك الحمد

## Our Lord! All praise is due only to You

*Meaning our Lord! We have praised You so accept it from us.*

# Sujood (The Prostration)

This is the most significant posture in the prayer. Uttering the below words in the state of prostration, by placing the face and forehead on to the ground, is an announcement of complete submission to Allah. This is why the Prophet Muhammad ﷺ urged us to make lots of supplications during this part of the prayer because it is most likely to be accepted.

سبحان ربي الأعلى

*Subhaana Rabbiyal A'alaa*

*How perfect is my Lord, the Most High*

سبحان ربي

**How perfect is my Lord**

*Meaning my Lord, who created me and sustains me, is sacred and free from all deficiencies and defects.*

الأعلى

**The Most High**

*This summons Allah's transcendence from all lowly things.*

# Tashahhud (The Sitting)

The words used in this posture can be divided into three distinct parts:

## First Part

التحيات لله والصلوات والطيبات، السلام عليك أيها النبي ورحمة الله وبركاته، السلام علينا وعلى عباد الله الصالحين، أشهد أن لا إله إلا الله، وأشهد أن محمدًا عبده ورسوله

*Athahiyyaatu lillaahi was-salawaatu wattayyibatu. Assalamu 'alaika ayyuhan-nabiyu warahmatullaahi wabarka'tuhu. Assalamu 'alaina wa'alaa 'ibaadillaahis saa'liheen. Ash'had'u alla ilaha illallahu wa ash'hadu anna Muhammadan abd'uhu wa rasooluh*

*All compliments, prayers, and good words are due to Allah. Peace be upon you, O Prophet, and the mercy of Allah and His blessings. Peace be on us and on the righteous servants of Allah. I bear witness that there is no deity worthy of worship except Allah, and I bear witness that Muhammad is His servant and His messenger*

التحيات لله

**All compliments are due to Allah**

*Meaning everything that indicates the glorification, transcendence, and greatness of Allah belong to Him alone. For example, bowing and prostrating are indications of*

*Allah's greatness and belong to Him alone. They cannot be performed for anyone other than Him.*

و الصلوات

## And prayers

*Meaning all supplications are made to Allah alone. Some have also said that it is in reference to the five daily prayers.*

و الطيبات

## And good words

*Meaning words that glorify, sanctify, and point to the greatness of Allah belong to Allah alone because He is deserving of it. For example, saying tasbeeh[2], takbeer, tahleel[3], etc.*

السلام عليك أيها النبي ورحمة الله وبركاته

## Peace be upon you, O Prophet, and the mercy of Allah and His blessings

*This is a supplication for peace, mercy, and blessings to be sent on the Prophet Muhammad ﷺ. It is a request to bestow **additional** mercy and blessings to that which he has already received.*

---

[2] Saying *Subhaan Allah*

[3] Saying *La ilaaha illa Allah*

السلام علينا وعلى عباد الله الصالحين

## Peace be on us and on the righteous servants of Allah

*Here we are supplicating for Allah's protection from all evil and that He keep us and all righteous servants of His on Islam until death. Some have also explained that here the worshiper is sending peace upon himself and upon every righteous servant of Allah, whether that servant be on earth or in the heavens.*

أشهد أن لا إله إلا الله

## I bear witness that there is no deity worthy of worship except Allah

*Meaning I bear with certainty that no one in the heavens or the earth deserves to be worshiped except Allah Almighty alone.*

وأشهد أن محمدًا عبده ورسوله

## And I bear witness that Muhammad is His servant and His messenger

*Meaning I bear with certainty that Muhammad ﷺ is Allah's messenger and worshiper. He was the best of worshipers to walk the face of the earth, a true servant of Allah.*

*The person here is also bearing witness that the Prophet ﷺ has delivered the message that was given to him by Allah.*

# Second Part

اللهم صل على محمد وعلى آل محمد، كما صليت على إبراهيم، وعلى آل إبراهيم إنك حميد مجيد، اللهم بارك على محمد وعلى آل محمد، كما باركت على إبراهيم، وعلى آل إبراهيم، إنك حميد مجيد

*Allaahumma salle 'alaa Muhammadin wa'alaa' aale Muhammadin kama sallaiyta 'alaa Ibraheema wa 'aAlaa Aale Ibraheema. Innaka Hameedum Majeed. Allaahumma baarik 'alaa Muhammadin wa 'alaa aale Muhammadin kama baarakta 'ala Ibraheema wa 'alaa Aale Ibraheema. Innaka Hameedum Majeed*

*O Allah, send prayers upon Muhammad and upon the family of Muhammad, as You sent prayers upon Abraham and the family of Abraham, You are indeed worthy of praise, full of glory. O Allah, bless Muhammad and the family of Muhammad as You blessed Abraham and the family of Abraham, You are indeed worthy of praise, full of glory*

اللهم صل على محمد

## O Allah, send prayers upon Muhammad

*Meaning O Allah, I ask you for every good and mercy for your messenger Muhammad ﷺ.*

وعلى آل محمد

## And upon the family of Muhammad

*Meaning send every good and mercy on his offspring, wives, and the progeny of Hashim and Al-Muttalib. They are all considered part of the family of the Prophet Muhammad ﷺ. Some scholars also hold the opinion that 'family' here is in reference to all of the followers of the Prophet ﷺ.*

كما صليت على إبراهيم، وعلى آل إبراهيم

## As You sent prayers upon Abraham and the family of Abraham

*Meaning in the same way, O Allah, You granted the Prophet Abraham and his family goodness and mercy.*

اللهم بارك على محمد

## O Allah, bless Muhammad

*Meaning O Allah increase him in the goodness of this life and the next.*

إنك حميد

## You are indeed worthy of praise

*Meaning You are, O Allah, indeed deserving of all sorts of praise and free from any imperfections.*

مجيد

## Full of glory

*Meaning O Allah for You is all glory, honor, and complete perfection.*

## Third Part

Here the worshiper can make any general supplications but those mentioned in the Qur'an and Sunnah are **preferred**. The most widely read are the following two:

### Supplication 1

اللهم إني أعوذ بك من عذاب جهنم ومن عذاب القبر ومن فتنة المحيا والممات ومن فتنة المسيح الدجال

*Allahumma inni a'udhu bika min 'adhabi jahannam, wa min 'adhabil-qabr, wa min fitnatil-mahya wal-mamat, wa min fitnatil-masihid-Dajjal*

*O Allah, I seek refuge in You from the torment of Hell, and I seek refuge in You from the torment of the grave, and I seek refuge in You from the trials of life and death, and I seek refuge in You from the tribulation of the Dajjal*

اللهم إني أعوذ بك

**O Allah, I seek refuge in You**

*Meaning I seek protection in You alone O Allah.*

من عذاب جهنم

**From the torment of Hell**

*This is in reference to the fire of Hell on Day of Resurrection.*

و من عذاب القبر

## And from the torment of the grave

*This is in reference to the punishment of the grave that occurs in the realm of **barzakh**, the time period between a person's death and the Day of Resurrection.*

و من فتنة المحيا و الممات

## And from the trials of life and death

*The 'trials of life' is in reference to anything that keeps the worshiper away from remembering Allah, worshiping Him, and distracts him from the afterlife.*

*The 'trials of death' is in reference to the questioning in the grave, therefore, the worshiper is asking Allah to keep him/her firm during that time.*

## Supplication 2

رب اجعلني مقيم الصلاة ومن ذريتي ربنا وتقبل دعاء. ربنا اغفر لي ولوالدي وللمؤمنين يوم يقوم الحساب

*Rabbi jalni muqimas salata wa min dhurriyyati rabbana wa taqabbal dua. Rabbana aghfirli waliwalidaiyya wa lil muminina yawma yaqumul hisab*

*My Lord, make me an establisher of prayer, and [many] from my descendants. Our Lord, and accept my supplication. Our*

*Lord, forgive me and my parents and the believers the Day
the account is established*

These two are verses from *Surah Ibraheem* (14:40-41) in the
Qur'an. Sh. Muhammad Ali Al-Sabuni explains the two
verses in his book of exegesis *Al-Tafseer Al-Waadhih
Al-Muyassar* as follows:

*"Meaning my Lord make me and my offspring among those
who preserve the salah. This is the best supplication a
believer can make for his children because the salah is a
shielded fortress for their faith and a fundamental pillar of the
religion. Prophet Abraham ﷺ ended his seven
supplications[4] by seeking forgiveness for himself, his
parents, and all believers until the Day of Resurrection, when
mankind will stand before the Lord of all the worlds."[5]*

---

[4] These two supplications were part of a list of seven supplications
Prophet Abraham made to Allah. They are all mentioned in Qur'an
14:35-41.

[5] Al-Sabuni, Muhammad Ali. *Al-Tafseer Al-Waadhih Al-Muyassar*, pg. 634

# Common Mistakes During Salah

The following is a list of common mistakes that Muslims make during the *salah*. Correcting these mistakes could help the worshiper increase and maintain his/her focus in the *salah*:

- **Not staying still** - Constantly fidgeting during *salah*, looking at a watch, fiddling with one's fingers or clothes, constantly scratching one's body parts, moving the feet, or other parts of the body restlessly are all things which must be avoided. When a Muslim stands before Allah, he/she should be still. Such actions only distract the worshiper from his prayer.

- **Reciting the words of *salah* too fast** - The worshiper should take his/her time when uttering the different words of *salah*. He/She should not be hasty by remembering that one is speaking to Allah, hence, he/she should be humble and full of awe.

- **Moving too quickly between postures** - Many Muslims perform their *salah* very quickly and they shift between different postures of *salah* as though they are crows pecking at food. A Muslim should remain calm and move between each posture slowly and with humbleness. The correct way to move between postures is to not do so until all the joints of the body have come to rest in that position.

- **Racing with the imam** - When praying behind an imam, a Muslim should **neither** move to the next posture **before** the imam, **with** the imam, nor should he delay it a long time **after** the imam. The correct way to follow the imam is to do so after the imam has reached the following posture and all his joints have come to rest in that position.

# Further Useful Resources on Salah

The following is a brief list of more resources a person can utilize to become acquainted with the words of *salah*, thereby, improving his/her focus and connection with Allah during the prayer:

**Youtube Videos (search for the titles on the site):**

- The Meaning of the Tashahhud by Sh. Abdul Nasir Jangda

- Tips to Improve Concentration in Salah by Sh. Mufti Menk

- Significance in the Different Postures of Salah by Sh. Yasir Qadhi

- Practical Steps to Develop Concentration (Kushoo') in Salah by Sh. Abdul Nasir Jangda

**Books and Articles (search for the titles on Google):**

- 33 Ways of developing Khushoo' in Salaah by Sh. Muhammad Salih al-Munajjid

- What Do We Say in Our Salah? By Umm Salih

Made in the USA
Middletown, DE
05 September 2024

60375460R00018